I0788119

TEN SIGNS OF CHEATER

BY: A. HIGHSMITH

INTRODUCTION: WELL FIRST LET ME SAY THAT THIS BOOK IS SOLELY OFF A 100-PEOPLE SURVEY. MEN AND WOMEN THAT WERE VICTIMS OF A CHEATING SPOUSE AND HOW THEY CAUGHT THEM WHEN I ASKED 100 WOMEN AND 100 MEN HOW THEY CAUGHT THEIR SPOUSE CHEATING. I TOOK ALL THE SIGNS AND THE ONES WITH THE HIGHEST PERCENTAGE. I USED THEM TO CREATE: THE TEN SIGNS OF A CHEATER. I AM ALSO ONE OF THE HUNDRED MEN THAT WAS QUESTIONED. IN THE PAST, I'VE BEEN TIED UP WITH A CHEATER A TIME OR TWO AND I ALWAYS CAUGHT THEM. G.I JOE SAID IT THE BEST "KNOWING

IS HALF THE BATTLE, BUT BEING OBSERVANT IS THE KEY. BUT BEING TOO OBSERVANT OR REACTING TO SOON WILL BLOW YOUR INVESTIGATION. SO JUST BECAUSE YOUR SPOUSE DOES ONE OR MAYBE TWO OF THESE SIGNS DOESN'T MEAN THAT THEY MAY BE A LOW-DOWN SCHEMING CHEAT. (BASTARDS!!) SOME PEOPLE DO HAVE WEIRD BUT INNOCENT BEHAVIOR. NOW IF THEY HAVE THREE OR MORE OF THESE SIGNS GOING ON. I'M SORRY TO SAY BUT CHANCES ARE VERY LIKELY THAT YOU ARE IN LOVE WITH

A CHEATER!! NOW BACK TO THE FIRST KEY, OBSERVATION. STUDY YOUR MATES BODY LANGUAGE. LIKE WHEN YOU KNOW FOR A FACT THAT THEY ARE LYING TO SOMEONE. LET'S SAY A RELATIVE CALL AND ASK YOUR SPOUSE TO BORROW SOME MONEY, BUT THIS RELATIVE IS KNOWN FOR NOT PAYING MONEY BACK. TAKING THE EASY WAY OUT, HE LIES. YOU KNOW FOR A FACT THAT YOUR SPOUSE HAS IT.

HUMANS ARE CREATURES OF HABIT. MEANING THAT WHATEVER TELL IT TELL SIGN THEY DO WHEN THEY TELL A LIE. WILL MORE THAN LIKELY BE THE SAME EVERY TIME THAT THEY ARE BEING UNTRUTHFUL. I HAVE A FRIEND THAT BLINKED HIS EYE LIDS RAPIDLY 3 OR 4 TIMES BEFORE HE STARTED HIS LIE. IT WAS HOW HE PROCESSED HIS PART OF THE BRAIN WHERE LIES ARE MADE. DIFFERENT PEOPLE HAVE MANNERISMS WHEN THEY LIE, VOICE TONE CHANGES. SOME PEOPLE VOICE GOES UP AN OCTAVE AND SOME GO LOWER. TAKING ON A CONVINCING TONE. YOU JUST MUST BE OBSERVANT AND STUDY YOUR PARTNER.

THE SAYING GOES; SCRATCH A LIE FIND A THIEF! WELL IF THEY WILL LIE THEN THEY WILL ALSO CHEAT. NOW BEFORE I TAKE YOU INTO THE SIGNS OF A CHEATER, LET ME SAY THIS. THIS BOOK WAS NOT WRITTEN TO BREAK UP RELATIONSHIPS, BECAUSE THEY ARE SOME PEOPLE THAT ARE WORTH TRYING TO WORK IT OUT WITH IF THEY ACKNOWLEDGE THEIR WRONGS AND THEY ARE WILLING TO CHANGE, AND ADMIT TO THE ERROR OF THEIR WAYS.

1.) THE MAD TEXTER

NOW THIS IS THE PERSON THAT PHONE IS ALWAYS SOUNDING OFF, YOU'D THINK THAT THEY RAN A BUSINESS THROUGH TEXTING. NOW BEWARE OF FACE BOOK BECAUSE PEOPLE WILL USE FACE BOOK AS AN OK STONE, SO BEWARE OF CONSTANT FACE BOOK DINGS (MESSAGE). MY

LAST GIRLFRIEND PHONE DINGED ALL THROUGH THE NIGHT AND AT THE POINT WHEN I COULDN'T BARE IT NO MORE I ASKED. "WHO IN THE WORLD KEEPS TEXTING YOU THIS TIME OF NIGHT?" SHE SAID WAS FROM A POST THAT SHE HAD RESPONDED TO EARLIER. NOW GIVING HER THE BENEFIT OF DOUBT I SAID OK. NOW THE NEXT NIGHT AND THE NIGHT AFTER THAT I BECAME SUSPICIOUS. I JUST KNEW BETTER. SHE TEXTS OR RECEIVED TEXT CONSTANTLY. I USED TO CALL HER PHONE THE HOT BOX. I'D BE LIKE BOY HERE WE GO AND SHE'D BE LIKE, "BOY STOP TRIPPING THAT'S MY COUSIN ASKING ABOUT

THE COOK OUT THIS WEEK END. LET ME SAY THIS YES PEOPLE DO LIKE TEXTING INSTEAD OF PICKING UP THE PHONE AND CALLING. THAT'S TRUE AND FOR THE MOST PART INNOCENT BUT THE MAD TEXTER TIES IN WITH A FEW OF THE OTHER SIGNS IN THIS BOOK. IF IT JUST SO HAPPENS THAT THEY DO THERE IS A POSSIBILITY THEY MAY BE A CHEATER.

2.) MASTER STORY TELLER

THIS IS THE PERSON THAT EVERY TIME THEY WERE SUPPOSED TO DO SOMETHING LIKE, TEXT BACK, CALL

YOU, MEET YOU SOME WHERE ETC. THIS PERSON HAS AN EXCUSE EVERY TIME THAT COMES WITH A STORY. NOW NORMALLY THINGS DO HAPPEN AND THEY JUST CAN'T DO WHATEVER IT WAS THAT THEY WERE SUPPOSED TO. HOWEVER, IF YOU ARE GETTING CONSTANT STORIES BEWARE. FOR INSTANCE, IF YOUR MATE WAS SUPPOSED TO COME OVER OR YOU ALL WERE SUPPOSED TO GO OUT BUT THEY DISAPPEARED AND WHEN YOU FINALLY TALK TO THEM THEY GIVE YOU A STORY LIKE. "BAE WHAT HAPPENED TO YOU?" "OH, I'M SORRY BUT SOMETHING CAME UP."

"OH, IS EVERYTHING ALRIGHT?" "YEAH IT WAS HORRIBLE HONEY." "WELL WHAT HAPPENED DEAR?" "WELL I WAS WALKING FLUFFY AND A GREAT BIG LION HAD ESCAPED FROM THE ZOO. IT JUMPS OUT OF THE BRUSH AT ME AND

FLUFFY TRIED TO DEFEND ME. FLUFFY WAS JUST TOO SMALL FOR THE LION, BUT FLUFFY JUST WOULDN'T LET THE LION GET TO ME. IT JUST SO HAPPENED THAT THEY WERE SEARCHING FOR THE LION AND ALREADY

IN THE NEIGHBORHOOD. THEY SPOTTED THE COMMOTION AND SAVED ME AND FLUFF'S LIFE BECAUSE I'M SURE THAT LION WOULD'VE KILLED US BOTH."

"WOW BABY"

"YES I HAD TO TAKE FLUFFY TO THE VET AND THEY HAD TO SOW HIS TAIL BACK ON" YES BEWARE OF CONSTANT STORIES AND EXCUSES. IF YOUR MATE GIVES YOU ENOUGH STORIES TO WRITE A BOOK. THEN YOU SHOULD BEWARE

3.) THE LOOKER/ THE MAD EYE BALLER.

THIS IS A DEAD GIVEAWAY FOR A CHEATER EVEN THOUGH IT MAY NOT NECESSARILY MEAN THAT THEY ARE CHEATING ON YOU. HOWEVER, IF YOU ARE IN A SERIOUS RELATIONSHIP, JUST THINK ABOUT WHY AND WHAT MUST THEY BE LOOKING FOR? PICTURE YOURSELF IN A CAR THAT YOU'RE NOT REALLY SATISFIED WITH. YEAH IT GETS YOU TO POINT A TO B BUT YOU JUST MAY BE INTERESTED IN ANOTHER CAR. NOW IF YOU ARE DRIVING DOWN A ROAD AND SEE A NICE-LOOKING CAR WITH A FOR SALE

SIGN ON IT. WHAT'S THE FIRST THING THAT PEOPLE SAY? "HMM, I WONDER WHAT THEY WANT FOR THAT CAR," THE LOOKER THOUGH IS WONDERING, HMM I WONDER IF SHE OR HE IS AVAILABLE. IF THE LOOKER IS NOT SATISFIED WITH WHO THEY ARE WITH AND MORE THAN LIKELY THEY ARE A PLAYER AND COULD BE JUST BE LOOKING TO MAKE A PLAY. ESPECIALLY IF THE PERSON THAT THEY ARE LOOKING AT GIVES THEM THE LOOK. NOW PLEASE PLEASE BE AWARE OF THE MAD EYE BALLER BECAUSE THEY WILL EYE BALL WHILE THEY ARE OUT WITH YOU IN PUBLIC. (OFF WITH THEIR HEAD!!" MEANING YOU START FIGURING HOW

TO EASE YOUR HEART DOWN FOR WHAT'S COMING IF YOU DON'T CUT THE CORD ON THAT RELATIONSHIP UNLESS YOU ARE A PLAYER TOO. THAT'S A BENEFICIAL RELATIONSHIP, THAT'S ANOTHER HORSE. THERE ARE INNOCENT EYE BALLERS. THE INCOGNITO EYE BALLER. THEY WILL LOOK BUT WON'T BUST A GRAPE, AND THERE IS ALSO SOME THAT WILL MAKE A BOTTLE OF WINE ON YOUR HIND PARTS TOO. THE INCOGNITO EYE BALLER IS A SNEAKER, HARDER TO CATCH. THIS WOULD BE THE PERSON THAT NEVER GIVES UP ALL THE DETAILS WHEN

YOU ASK THEM WHERE THEY BEEN OR WHO THEY WERE WITH ETC.

4.) SILENT ASSASSIN/ PHONE ON CREEP MODE.

EVERY ASSASSIN MOVIE I WATCHED, THE ASSASSIN'S WHOLE THING WAS TO MOVE IN SILENCE, AT NIGHT THEY WORE DARK CLOTHING. TO OPERATE WITHOUT BEING DETECTED, UNNOTICED, NO WITNESSES AND MOST IMPORTANTLY SILENTLY. IN A RELATIONSHIP, I BELIEVE THAT A SILENT PHONE ALL THE TIME IS A GIVEAWAY. IF YOU'RE NOT IN THE MOVIES OR SOMEWHERE WHERE THAT YOUR PHONE IS REQUIRED TO BE ON SILENT. WHEN YOUR MATE

PHONE IS NOT EVEN ON VIBRATE. BOY WHAT IS THE PURPOSE FOR THAT. MY LAST MATE KEPT HER PHONE ON SILENT AND WHEN SHE WENT TO SLEEP SHE WOULD PUT IT UNDER HER PILLOW, WHOA! WHERE THEY DO THAT AT? THE PURPOSE FOR THAT WAS SO THAT I WOULD NOT MOLEST HER PHONE WHILE SHE WAS SLEEP. MUST'VE BEEN SOME JUICY STUFF IN THERE. THIS ONE TIES IN TO THE NEXT SIGN WHICH IS THE PHONE PROTECTOR. MOST TIMES THIS PERSON WILL WAIT UNTIL YOU ARE OCCUPIED THEN SNEAK OFF TO THE BATHROOM AND CHECK THEIR MESSAGES. TWO MORE THINGS, ONE

IS A RED FLAG, WHICH IS: IF YOU'RE OUT OF THE ROOM OR HOUSE AND WHEN YOU WALK IN THEY CLOSE THEIR SCREEN. (PUSH THE HOME BUTTON) NORMALLY THIS IS NOT OUT OF THE ORDINARY BUT IF YOU NOTICE THAT IT'S A CONSTANT THING THAT THEY CLOSE THEIR SCREEN OUT EVERY TIME YOU WALK IN. THEN HMMM GO FIGURE. THE OTHER ONE I CALL THE CUFF GAME. IF YOU AROUND, CLOSE BY THEM AND THEY GET A TEXT. THEY WILL HAVE THEIR HAND SORT OF CUFFING THE PHONE AND THE SCREEN SLIGHTLY TURNED AWAY SO THAT YOU CANNOT SEE WHO OR WHAT THE PHONE SAYS SO BEWARE OF THE CUFF GAME, BUT

MOST IMPORTANTLY THE SILENT ASSASSIN!

5.) BEHOLD THE PHONE SCREEN PROTECTOR. /OUT YOUR REACH ALWAYS.

THIS WILL BE SHORT AND SWEET. THIS IS THE PERSON THAT NEVER FAILS TO PUT THEIR PHONE FACE DOWN WHEN THEY ARE AROUND YOU AFTER RECEIVING A CALL OR TEXT. THIS IS ALSO THE PERSON THAT IN A CAR WITH YOU OR ANYWHERE WILL TRY TO 75% OF THE TIME KEEP THE PHONE OUT OF YOUR REACH. JUST IN CASE YOU DECIDE TO GRAB IT ONE DAY WHEN IT GOES OFF AND ASKED

WHO IS TEXTING YOU? ON CELL PHONES WHEN A TEXT OR CALL COMES IN, MOST TIMES IT WILL SHOW THE TEXT AND WHO IT IS FROM. THE PROTECTOR MUSTN'T ALLOW YOU TO SEE WHO IS CALLING OR TEXTING, IF THEY ARE NOT CHEATING THEN THERE SHOULDN'T BE ANYTHING TO HIDE. LET'S NOT FORGET THE OLD LOCKED PHONE STORY. NOW COMING INTO A FRESH RELATIONSHIP, IT IS UNDERSTANDABLE, BUT AFTER SIX MONTHS THERE SHOULDN'T BE ANY LOCKED PHONES. TO ME LOCKS ARE TO KEEP THINGS PROTECTED.

6.) MR. & MRS. POPULARITY

I USED TO BE WITH THIS PERSON AND I'VE BEEN IN A RELATIONSHIP WITH SOMEONE THAT WAS VERY POPULAR. IT SEEMED LIKE EVERYWHERE WE WENT SOME ONE KNEW HER. "HEY TINA!" THEY SAY WALKING UP BUT THEN WHEN THEY'D SEE THE LOOK IN MY EYES. THEIR WHOLE-BODY LANGUAGE WOULD CHANGE. THEN IT WOULD BECOME A SHORT TIGHT CONVERSATION IF YOU KNOW WHAT I MEAN. NOW WHILE I'M ON THIS SUBJECT LET'S DISCUSS YOUR PARTNERS BODY LANGUAGE AGAIN YOU MUST BE AN OBSERVATION EST, BECAUSE THE BODY TALKS, AND

MOST TIMES SCREAMS. IF YOU'RE NOT LISTENING YOU WILL BE LATE IN THE GAME. MAN, OH MAN THIS PERSON HAD SO MANY COUSINS. AFTER LIKE, THE FIFTIETH COUSIN. "I SAID DAMN YOU SURE GOT A LOT OF COUSINS!" EVERYWHERE WE WENT SOMEONE KNEW HER AND HER PHONE WAS ALWAYS GOING OFF. FACE BOOK WAS DINGING ALL THE TIME. "YOU SHOW GOT A LOT OF COUSIN BABES!!!" "YEAH WE A BIG FAMILY." WAS HER REPLY. AGAIN, MOST OF THESE WILL TIE INTO EACH OTHER, A COMPOUND SIGN IS A RED FLAG.

7.) HOUDINI/ THE MASTER OF THE DISAPPEARING ACT.

YOU EVER NOTICED LIKE DURING WORK HOURS, YOUR MATE OR SOMEONE THAT YOU MAY BE JUST MEETING. WILL TEXT LIKE CRAZY. JUST LIKE CLOCKWORK EVERY TIME YOU TEXT THEM THEY HIT RIGHT BACK. THEN LATER IT'S LIKE THEY LEFT THE PLANET. YOU TEXT THEM AND WHEN THEY DO TEXT BACK ITS VERY DELAYED OR NOT AT ALL. LATER WHEN THEY DO TEXT OR CALL. MORE THAN LIKELY IT WILL TIE INTO ANOTHER SIGN, LIKE THE MASTER STORY TELLER. OH YEAH, IT'LL BE A STORY OR AN EXCUSE,

BET YOUR LONG-LEGGED LIFE ON THAT. "OH, I'M SORRY I FELL ASLEEP" THAT'S ONE AND ANOTHER IS, "SORRY BABY MY PHONE DIED AND I DIDN'T HAVE MY CHARGER." NOW THESE THINGS DO HAPPEN BUT IF ITS CONSTANT, SOMEBODY LYING!!

8.) THE ANGRY CAMPER/ THE ACCUSER.

THIS IS THE PERSON THAT NO MATTER WHAT YOU TRY TO DO TO MAKE THEM HAPPY. YOU CANNOT. THEY MAY BE HAPPY MOMENTARILY

BUT SOMETHING IS GOING TO RUB THEM THE WRONG WAY. THEY WILL

FIND SOMETHING TO COMPLAIN ABOUT. THIS TIES INTO THE TENTH SIGN. YOU'LL READ THAT ONE SHORTLY. IT'S ALWAYS SOMETHING ABOUT YOU THAT THEY GOT TO REMARK ON, OR HAVE A PROBLEM WITH. THIS OCCURS MORE IN MARRIAGES

THEN REGULAR RELATIONSHIPS. THE PERSON IS MORE THAN LIKELY ANGRY BECAUSE THEY'RE SO CLOSE TO BEING STUCK IN A MARRIAGE. A LOT OF PEOPLE GET MARRIED THINKING THAT THIS IS THE ONE. A COUPLE OF YEARS OR EVEN MONTHS DOWN THE LINE. THEY HAVE A RUDE AWAKENING. WAKE UP ONE

MORNING, REALIZING THAT THIS IS NOT THE ONE, AND ANGRY FROM THAT POINT ON. THAT OLD BALL AND CHAIN THAT'S HOOKED TO THAT FINGER ISN'T ENOUGH TO STOP THEM FROM TRYING TO FIND HAPPINESS BY SNEAKING AND CHEATING. ALSO, BEWARE OF THE ACCUSER AND THE STALKER. THESE PEOPLE ARE THE ONES THAT ALWAYS ACCUSE YOU OF SOMETHING

OR SUSPECTS SOMETHING. THEY WATCH AND LISTEN. FOLLOW YOU, COME WHERE YOU SUPPOSED TO BE AND ASK YOUR FRIENDS FOR INFORMATION. CALL YOUR JOB TO MAKE SURE YOU AT WORK. ASK YOURSELF WHY IS THAT WHEN YOU

BE DOING EVERYTHING HONESTLY AND YOU'RE NOT A CHEAT. WELL IF THEY ARE CLOCKING YOUR EVERY MOVE THEN THEY SHOULD KNOW THAT YOU ARE PLAYING IT STRAIGHT. NOW I WAS ALWAYS TOLD THAT IF YOU SCRATCH A LIE YOU'LL FIND A CHEAT. A PERSON THAT ALWAYS ACCUSE YOU OF CHEATING OR STEALING IS THE ONE THAT MUST BE WATCHED ESPECIALLY IF YOUR INNOCENT. THIS STRATEGY IS TO KEEP YOU OF BALANCE,

KEEPING YOU AGGRAVATED SO THAT YOU WILL NOT FOCUS ON HOW THEY ARE MOVING. THE THING IS TO ALWAYS BE OBSERVANT BUT NOT

OVERLY OBSERVANT WHERE THEY WILL KNOW THAT YOU'RE WATCHING AND PAYING ATTENTION. THERE FOR MOVE LIKE AN ASSASSIN, UNSEEN OR NOTICED...

9.) THE GIFT BARER/ BEHOLD I COME BARING GIFTS. THIS IS THE PERSON THAT WILL SPOIL YOU. LET YOU HAVE YOUR WAY, AND LET ME TELL YOU WHY. A PERSON THAT IS BLINDED BY GIFTS CANNOT SEE PASS THE GIFTS. ALWAYS GETTING YOUR WAY IS A WAY TO KEEP YOU OFF BALANCE. EVERY SPORT THAT I KNOW OF, YOU MUST BE BALANCED TO PLAY. THE GIFT BARER WILL HAVE YOU

THINKING THAT YOU CAN GET ANYTHING THAT YOU WANT. LIKE PUTTY IN YOUR HANDS,

YEAH RIGHT! JUST BEWARE OF THE GIFT BARER. A MISSED DATE, UNEXPLAINED ABSENCES ETC. I CAN ASSURE YOU THAT THERE WILL BE A GIFT FOLLOWING IT. I WON'T SAY EVERY TIME BUT SOME LIKE BEING SPOILED. THE AUDIENCE THAT THIS IS BOOK IS REACHING OUT TOO IS THE ONES THAT DON'T LIKE BEING CHEATED ON... THIS SIGN WILL TIE INTO THE

MASTER STORY TELLER ALONG

WITH THE DISAPPEARING ACT.

10.) DR. JEKYLL & MR HYDE / SPLIT PERSONALITY

NOW FINALLY. THE WHO ARE YOU REALLY OR WHAT PERSONALITY ARE YOU WHEN YOU'RE NOT AROUND ME. IF YOU'RE IN A RELATIONSHIP WITH SOMEONE THAT CHANGES PERSONALITIES RIGHT IN FRONT OF YOUR EYES. BOY IS YOUR HANDS FULL, AND MOST IMPORTANTLY BE CAREFUL. MAY BE A SERIAL KILLER IN THERE SOMEWHERE. MOST OF

THESE CASES MAY BE (DID) MEDICAL TERM THEY ARE MORE THAN ONE PERSON, JUST BE CAREFUL BECAUSE THERE IS NO TELLING WHAT ROLL THEY MAY TAKE ON WHEN NOT AROUND YOU.

WELL I WOULD LIKE TO SAY THANKS FOR READING MY BOOK. I WOULD ALSO LIKE TO MENTION THAT PEOPLE HAVE PROBLEMS, SOME WILL ADMIT AND SOME WILL DENY THE FACT. THE

ONES THAT ARE SINCERE AND ADMIT THAT THEY HAVE A PROBLEM AND WILLING TO TRY AND GET BETTER ARE THE ONES THAT YOU CAN WORK WITH. NOW THERE ARE A LOT OF OTHER SIGNS BUT MINE ARE SOLELY BASED ON THE CELL PHONE AND THERE AREN'T MANY PEOPLE THAT WILL TRAVEL ANYWHERE WITHOUT THEIR PHONE. I CALL IT THE FLY ON THE WALL. WELL THIS IS ENOUGH INFO FOR YOU TO KNOW WHETHER IF YOU ARE BEING PLAYED LIKE A FIDDLE. HOPEFULLY THOUGH YOU'RE NOT BUT WE KNOW BETTER... REMEMBER DOESN'T NOTHING COME TO A SLEEPER BUT A DREAM.............................THE END

www.ingramcontent.com/pod-product-compliance
Lightning Source LLC
Chambersburg PA
CBHW050809240726
48654CB00019B/621